Balls

Written by
Melanie Davis Jones

Illustrated by Linda Bronson

jCO

Children's Press®
A Division of Scholastic Inc.
New York • Toronto • London • Auckland • Sydney
Mexico City • New Delhi • Hong Kong
Danbury, Connecticut

To my favorite ballplayers: Randy, Trent, Justin, and Cameron
—M.D.J.

For C.R.L.
—L.B.

Reading Consultants

Linda Cornwell
Literacy Specialist

Katharine A. Kane
Education Consultant
(Retired, San Diego County Office of Education and San Diego State University)

Library of Congress Cataloging-in-Publication Data

Jones, Melanie Davis.
  Balls / written by Melanie Davis Jones ; illustrated by Linda Bronson.
      p. cm.—(Rookie reader)
Summary: Rhyming text introduces the many types of balls and how they
are used.
  ISBN 0-516-22596-0 (lib. bdg.)   0-516-26967-4 (pbk.)
  [1. Balls (Sporting goods)—Fiction. 2. Stories in rhyme.] I. Bronson,
Linda, ill. II. Title. III. Series.
  PZ8.3.J7535 Bal 2002
  [E]—dc21
                              2001008322

CHILDREN'S PRESS, AND A ROOKIE READER®, and associated logos are trademarks
and or registered trademarks of Grolier Publishing Co., Inc. SCHOLASTIC and associated
logos are trademarks and or registered trademarks of Scholastic Inc.
1 2 3 4 5 6 7 8 9 10 R 11 10 09 08 07 06 05 04 03 02

Balls roll.

3

Balls spin.

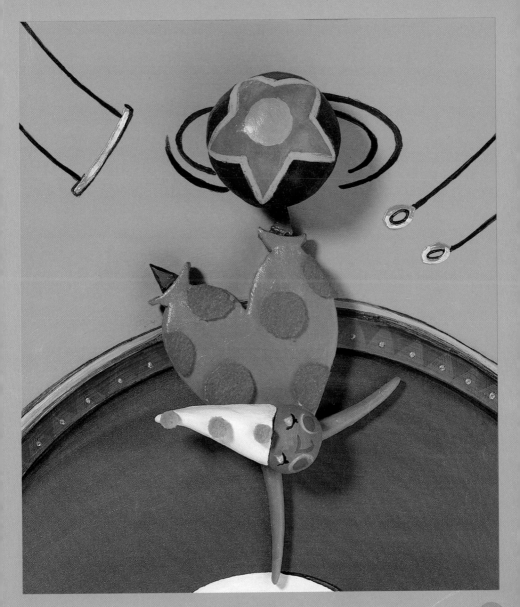

Balls knock down bowling pins.

Balls zoom.
Balls fly.

Balls pop up to the sky.

**Balls bounce.
Balls soar.**

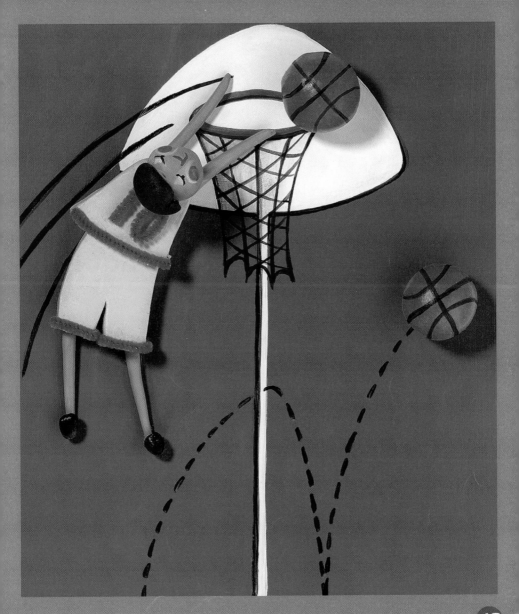

13

Balls go in the net to score.

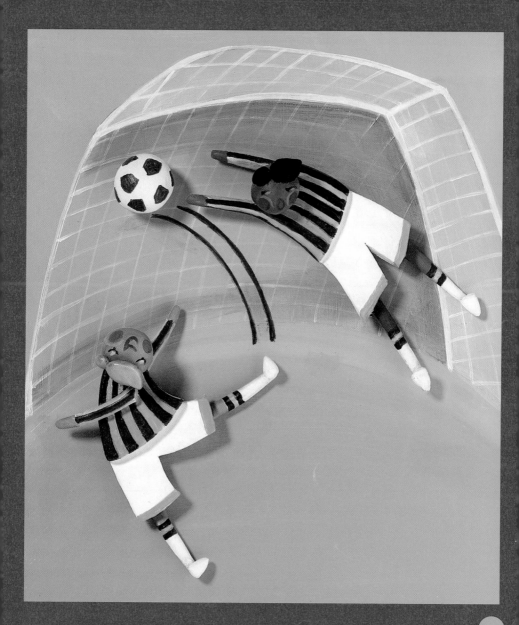

Balls go up.
Balls come down.

Count how many balls are round.

Balls are big.
Balls are small.

Count how many balls in all.

23

Word List (29 words)

· ·

all	come	in	roll	spin
are	count	knock	round	the
balls	down	many	score	to
big	fly	net	sky	up
bounce	go	pins	small	zoom
bowling	how	pop	soar	

About the Author

Melanie Davis Jones is a writer and an elementary school teacher. She lives in Warner Robins, Georgia, with her husband, Randy, and their three sons. She spends much of her time running to baseball games, soccer games, basketball games, and bowling alleys. This is her first Rookie Reader.

About the Illustrator

Linda Bronson is the illustrator of several acclaimed children's books, including *Teatime with Emma Buttersnap* and *The Circus Alphabet.* She lives in upstate Connecticut with her husband Charlie, their cat Tazzy, and their rabbit Mr. Nubs.